Underlying Premises

ALSO BY J.T. LEDBETTER

Plum Creek Odyssey

Gethsemani Poems

Voices and Echoes

Voyages

Underlying Premises

Poems by

J.T. LEDBETTER

First published by Lewis Clark Press 2010

10 9 8 7 6 5 4 3 2 1

Library of Congress Cataloging-in-Publication Data
Ledbetter, J.T.
Underlying Premises / by J. T. Ledbetter
p. cm.
ISBN 978-0-911015-61-4
I. Underlying Premises II. Poetry III. Literature-Poetry IV. California Authors-Poetry V. Ledbetter J.T.

Printed in the United States of America
Set in Minion Pro
Designed by Kimberly Verhines

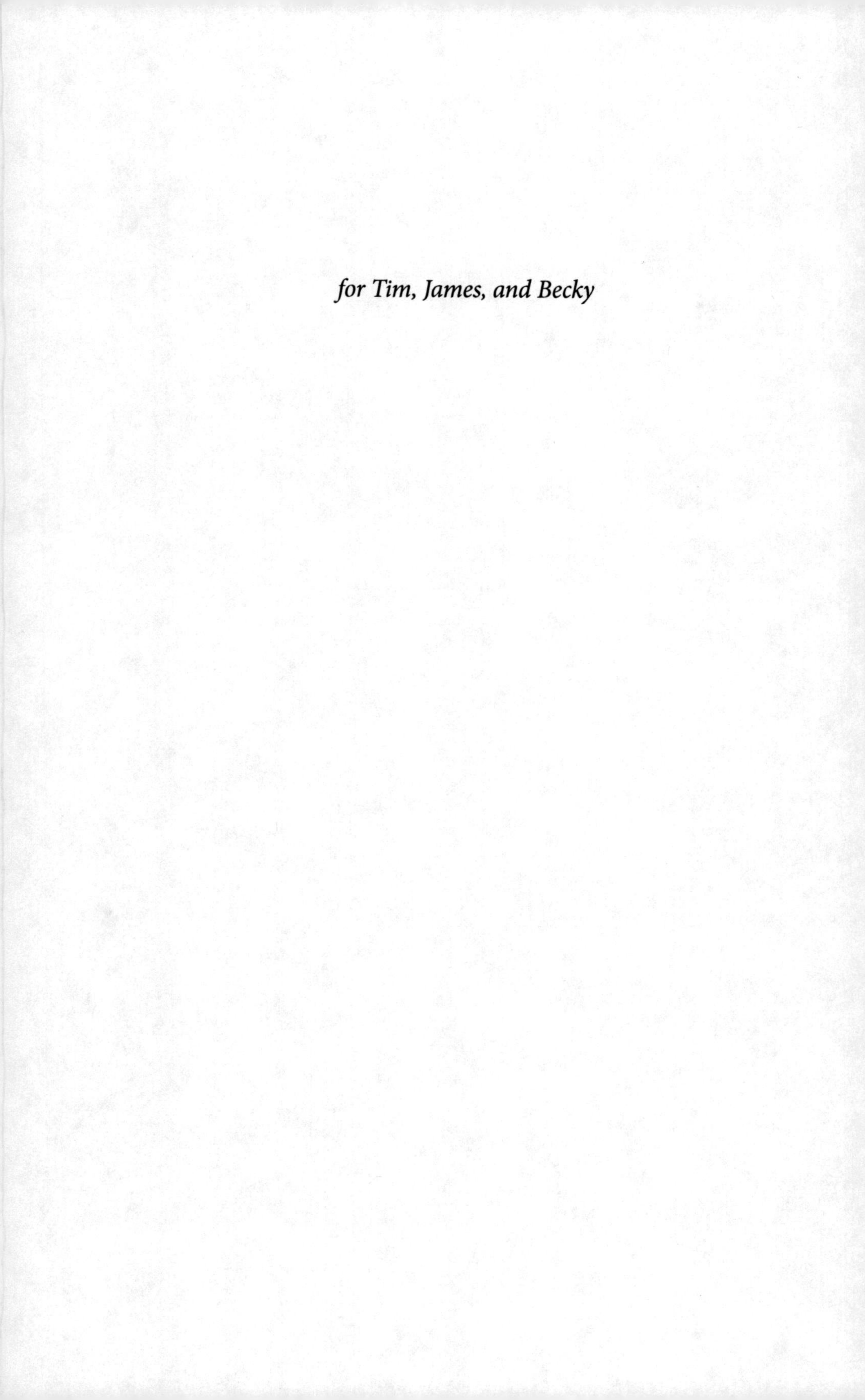

for Tim, James, and Becky

ACKNOWLEDGMENTS

THE ATLANTA REVIEW: “The Foxes at the Old Irish Cemetery”
ASHVILLE POETRY REVIEW: “Kentucky Spring”
ASPHODEL: “That Slight Edge of Beauty”
BAYOU: “Ice”
THE BIG MUDDY: “The Hard Illinois Ground”
BIRMINGHAM POETRY REVIEW: “owl”; “pond”
BRYANT LITERARY REVIEW: “The Red Chiffon”
THE CRESSET: “Blue Lantern Motel”; “Winter on Meadow Pond”
DEFINED PROVIDENCE: “Rain”
THE LAUREL REVIEW: “The Plow and the Field”
THE MACGUFFIN: “Watchers”
MARGIE: “News”
NATURAL BRIDGE: “When Aunt Eff Came to Visit”
THE NEW YORK QUARTERLY: “October”; “Girls in their Summer Dresses”; “Van Doren's Snake”
NEBRASKA REVIEW: “Like Country Women”
OBERON: “A Lady of Unspoken Graces”
PLEIADES: “When the Sun Went Down”
POETRY: “My Father's Voice”
POETRY EAST: “Like a White Bird Rising”
RATTLE: “Crossing Shoal Creek”; “Grandmother”
SALT FLATS REVIEW: “Something Different”; “Millay at the Mall (for Ted)”
THE SEWANEE REVIEW: “Under the Chinaberry Tree”
SOU'WESTER: The First Pale Light of Spring”; “In the Blue Iris of Early Morning”; “Bond County Funeral”
THE SOW'S EAR: “Country Women”; “Baptism”
THE TEXAS REVIEW: “A Man & Woman and a Dog with Pups”
STEAM TICKET: “Zoo Story”
THE TOLEDO REVIEW: “What They Didn't Say”
VISIONS: “In a Way You Loved”
WAR, LITERATURE and the ARTS: “Fire Fight”
XANADU: “Last Letter from Rose”
ZYZZYVA: “Morning/Greenville, Illinois”

CONTENTS

...the long return through night-time roads
across the mooned or unmooned sleeping land,
the mare's feet like slow silk in the dust...
–Faulkner, THE HAMLET

The wide ripe fields, the whole country,
seemed like a sleeping garden. One trod the dusty roads softly,
not to disturb the deep slumber of the world.
–Cather, A LOST LADY

The Plow and the Field

From the swing on the old wide-board porch
she listened to thunder rolling in Turley's Woods
and watched him pull the plow from the barn
where cows moved against their stanchions,
their thick breath puffs of cloud in the darkness.
She raised her hand against the setting sun
as he worked the field, and touched her leg
as he lifted the plowshare out of the furrow, feeling
his weight against it as he eased into the earth,
rocking up and down from furrow to furrow.
He watched the woman on the porch, her bare legs
shining in the dust, felt the length of her
on the swing, and took his hands off the plow
and slid them up her bare hot legs and felt
her sudden breath on his face as he eased her
backwards, smelling her thick hair in his face,
and in the movement of the plow felt the rhythm
of the swing carry them from furrow to furrow
where the rich earth parts and receives the seed,
rocking back and forth on the swing
smelling of dirt and sweat as field, plow, and swing
blurred in the grip of shoulders, buttocks,
furrowing the light from the humid sky as wind rustled
the bougainvillea above them and brought rain,
cooling the hot rich field where he stood,
the plow leaning in the furrow, catching fire
in last light.

The First Pale Light of Spring

When she woke in the first pale light of spring
she woke him and pointed to the corner
where the cradle caught the light through
the heavy curtains. She raised the window,
letting the fresh smells into the room.
Machinery rusted in the fields
and the empty silo rose above the thorn trees.
"Too bad it's a girl," he said at last.
She stood at the window and did not speak,
though there was much she meant to say--
something about the rain and long winters,
and her good clothes boxed in the root cellar
with the clean jars and eggs, and the dark
farm silence between them. But she knew
he was thinking of his breakfast of hot biscuits
and gravy and the old dog cracking her bones
on the gunny sack behind the stove,
waiting to go with him to the fields.

Thunder rolled in the bottoms as he swung
his feet out and walked stiffly toward the stairs,
curling his toes from the cold floor.
"She won't be help to me here. You'll have
to teach her something." His voice ballooned
up the stairwell and echoed in the bare rooms.
"Oh, I will," she whispered. "I will teach
her something!" And she pressed her body
full against the cold window as the farm
appeared and disappeared in the rain
and her face stared back from the greening fields.

Like Country Women

After a week of wind she took to standing by a long window
that looked over the garden and to the creek that ran through
the small copse of alders near the barn, and when the rains began
she took her book to the window niche and opened it on her lap
and sat looking out at the swollen stream as it raised itself over
the grassy banks and flooded the garden, finding each furrow
with fingers of water that opened and closed like a hand.

If he had come to her then it might have mattered.
If he had asked about the book or brought her, laughing,
a flower from the upper garden where they raised the earth
on rock from the dry stream bed the day she spread
her new dress around her on the warm grass and smelled
the thick scent of cut hay and damp earth.

But the days changed then and like country women, she changed
into the dress her mother made for her and carried the buckets
up the steps to the bathroom, and held the light in the barn
as they moved among the heavy cows with the thick medicine
to save the new calf, smelling the heavy sweet smell of milk
on the mother who laid her weight against her calf as if to press
life back into it.

And when the first snows banked against the root-cellar door
she wondered at the absence of any sound at all, and watched
the men go over the hill, leaving black marks in the white,
their shoulders hunched over in the cold, the wind drifting snow
into their footprints behind them as if they had suddenly appeared
in the snow and moved slowly into the dark trees with no sign
or sound to show they were men.

But no one asked her about what she saw or what she felt.
They left her to the cold room and ate in the kitchen

around the long table near the stove, silently, hunkered over
their biscuits and gravy and their coffee, their hats and hoods
still on their heads, ice on the bristles of their beards.

It was at night that she saw it all, knew she was there,
as the horses and cows were there, as the furniture with
the drop cloths were there, and that she had as little voice
or dream. When the house was asleep, and she stood by
the window and watched the moon catch in the plum tree
orchard, she knew the fox was moving through the frozen
garden, carefully lifting his slender legs in and out of the
melting snow, growling at the new ice in the ruts from
the wagon that brought the seed and bulbs she asked for.

Tomorrow she would plant them after digging up
the dark earth where she could. The men would laugh at her
there in the wet garden, telling her it was too soon,
too early for that, and they would shoulder their bright axes
and go to the deep woods where she would hear the sharp crack
of them biting into the ash and oak. Still she would sit there
in her garden and work her hands into the hard dirt, dropping
the seed carefully into the ground, covering it and patting down
the rich earth, watching him go with the men, not looking back,
wanting to lay her body down in the dark earth, in the narrow
furrow with the seed, feeling the dampness rise into her body,
smelling the honeysuckle on the broken trellis, her hands
working the cold earth, drawing spring into them.

Summer Girls

Summer girls flit like moths
over the Courthouse lawn,
country boys stand around.
Summer girls dance all night
on the hardwood platform
set up on the courthouse lawn.
Older folks watch from Bridey's
Cafe across the street and talk
of when they danced all night
beneath the spreading maples
and who they did or did not kiss.
In winter light they wait for summer,
lasting on memories.
But the Courthouse is ice
and the maples bare,
their memories cold as the fire
where they rock, remembering
who they did or did not kiss
as winter grasses hiss and hiss.

A Long Night Before Morning
(Greenville, Illinois)

Morning is in the trees in the upper garden you raised
on the rocky field and worked last summer,
and soon it will slide down the smooth alders into the pond,
waking the geese who stayed the winter with us.

From the kitchen window, I watch the old horse come up
from the fields for her carrots and oats,--and when the heat rises
shimmering and wet, I'll turn the cows into the pasture,
their bags swaying comically as they go in a line to the creek
where they will chew their cud in the cool water.

The rest of the day will go without notice, full of lists
saying to stay busy. Watch the weather, one said. Mornings will be best.
But after the last words by the new grave,
and the pressure of their bodies against me, there is still
the awful silence in the house, and a long night before morning.

When the Sun Went Down
(Greenville, Illinois)

When the sun went down people walked home
through Turley's Woods, stopping at the graves
hidden by oaks and elms and redbud trees.
"It will make a fine lake," the town man said.
"Not a soul will be bothered in their deep dark sleep."
No one took the money, and no one swam there;
then children did,-- and others heard of a lake
where a town had been and come to drink lemonade
on Sundays and men stand quiet in the shallows,
pants rolled up over white legs, their church hats
over their eyes. When the sun goes down they wake
the elderly and fold umbrellas and drive down the dirt road
to the highway, leaving the clear blue lake where someone swims
in the echo of sun on the water hiding the oaks and elms
and the redbud trees, and the town unbothered in its deep dark sleep.

My Father's Voice

In the winter my father worked the big horses
in the fields hauling out the stumps
as I ran along the furrows where ice
held the dead stalks stiff and straight
in the hard ground, and at night,
when the steam rose off the sweating backs
of the team, he moved among the harnesses
and sweet-smelling hay in the dark barn,
talking softly to them as their wet hides
rippled beneath his hands.

Later, when my brother's breathing eased
in our room beneath the eaves,
I went to the window and pressed myself
against the cold glass and watched the farm
appear and disappear in the rain,
and my father's voice came up the stairs
like thunder a long way off.

Now, when trees are wet and bent
against the windows, our children come
to our bed and press their warm bodies against us
wanting stories, and fall asleep with rain sluicing
through the rain gutters, the team coming up
from the fields, lifting their heavy legs
in and out of the wet grass, their coats glistening
like jewels in the mist, my father driving them,
his voice rising and falling in the cold air.

In the Cataloochee
(The Great Smokies)

-- in memory of my father

Deep inside the timber water flows down through
the hardwood trees, washing the ground clean,
tumbling over Rhododendron and berries to the valley
where you stand, a foot inside the forest, waiting.

There are no signs here. No coffee houses or televisions.
You cannot know about missiles fired or spaceships floating.
You only know the first step inside the dark woods is forever.

No one knows where you have gone because your footprints are gone
in soft ground where trickles of water find them and fill them,
leaving small pools known only to bears. It is not important
for you to know where you are or where you are going,

or that night is closing in, and water rushes past you over rocky ledges,
laving your body in a cool mist, and you breathe, easily,
listening to the night sounds and the water, until even your heart slows

and the blood in your veins leaps from stream to stream and the memory
of your life changes into green and wet and mist and smell and you become
a nurse log where ferns crack the chrysalis of your body, spreading
graceful tendrils, touching face and chest, breathing with you as vines twine
about your feet and legs, moving upward until your hair and fingertips grow
into the earth, touching the life you knew was there,
knowing it was waiting for you to just lie down on the ground and breathe,
holding the last breath inside until your eyes close, and the covering mist
becomes your evening prayer and birth-breath.

The Hard Illinois Ground
(southern Illinois)

My mother cried when we left the farm,
but my father hunched himself over the wheel
and started around the white-rock road to the highway.
"We forgot the cow," he said. " Go back and shoot her.
Then get in the truck or we won't make Albuquerque."

I found her behind the barn twisting her neck beneath the wire
to get at the new grass, her lower jaw working and rowing,
her long tongue raising clouds of flies that settled around her tight bag.
Her front legs buckled with the shot and she went down,
but she was not dead. My father cursed and got out of the truck
and walked stiff-legged toward me, but then her eyes went glassy
and her back legs kicked once as flies settled on the warm milk
dribbling from her distended teats onto the hard Illinois ground.

The Stream That Runs Through Turley's Woods

When she found the mushrooms beneath the rotting hemlock tree she threw down her basket and spread her skirt on the leaves and cooled her feet in the stream that runs through Turley's Woods. When he saw her he stopped on the bridge and watched her lift one leg and then the other, her skirt falling about her hips. He thought he should call out to her, then was afraid lest she scream or think he meant her harm; so he stood still, half in shadow, and watched her stand and in one easy movement shed the skirt, lifting her slender legs out and away, kicking the skirt with her foot. Something moved deep inside him there on the bridge beneath the overhanging boughs. He gripped the railing until the old wood crumbled and drifted on the dark water, but he said nothing, did nothing to attract her attention. Her white blouse was flung over her head and he thought he heard her singing as she stepped into the stream and caught her breath at the sudden cold water swirling about her naked legs and hips. And he watched her standing there and heard the song she sang and loved her more than anything he had ever known and knew he would have to speak or move before the white flower inside him cracked the chrysalis of the person standing on the bridge, a person he didn't know, a man lunging over the rain into the water making sounds he couldn't know or say, his clothes rising and falling by themselves, his mouth working in feeble incoherent speech, flailing through the shallow water toward her, naked and beautiful, her shoulders turning toward him, her hair catching fire in last light.

When Aunt Eff Came to Visit
(for Bill and Jim)

When Aunt Eff came to visit we were told to sit straight
and not ask questions about the fur she wore, but when we saw
the two beady eyes resting on her shoulder we cried
and were sent to bed where we wondered who shot it and why
and if it had babies that day when it flashed its brush
in Turley's Woods, its eyes red and fierce in the dark.

That night my Aunt's brightly-rouged face hovered
over me and the doctor talked low to my mother in the hall
and said I would not last, that the weather had done it,
but that he knew a man who wanted to sell a casket
that was lined with red and real nice, and my mother told him
to shut up and get out and gave me lemonade, while Bill
and Jim watched from the shadows, and my mother sang
a song until my father got home and she told him I was dying
and he said to let him know and went into the silo with the dog
to kill rats. So the next morning, when it was still dark,
and I came down for breakfast, my mother cried and hugged me
and said to pray, but my father was already pulling on his boots
to plow the bottoms, and as my mother sang in the kitchen
I watched him go past the upper garden where the song bird
watched with one bright eye from the moon-rinsed trees.

Sunday Dinner
(Alton, Illinois)

My mother told me two foreign sisters took in dry cleaning
upstairs over the grocery store but never took me with her,
but one day my father took me and told me to look at the
magazines while he went upstairs with Opolo and Anomolie
to look at their new wall paper. That night my mother gave me
another chicken wing and asked me where I went. Until that
moment I did not know plates could float along with words
and eyes and mouths open wide with no sound coming out,
but when the plates fell, the words and chairs fell with them
and my mother walked into the bedroom and my father went
outside and sat under the big elm and yelled that he was going
to go to California where the gold was and I ate the breasts and legs
and gave the old dog the neck while she was eating everything
on the floor, and when my mother came back I showed her one
of the magazines from the dry cleaning store and she went back into
the bedroom and came out with a baseball bat and the dog ran out
and I sat still until she banged through the screen door and then
the dog came back in and we started on the mashed potatoes and gravy.

In the Blue Iris of Early Morning

In the blue iris of early morning I raise on an elbow
to listen to the singing from the river
where a camp meeting has begun...
the heavy dotted-swiss curtains billow into my room
and the preacher's voice rises and falls with the whistle
from the night train to Cincinnati burrowing through Kentucky
heading north into Ohio...something is happening there in the river
something is happening--someone is being baptized
and maybe a choir wears white standing with the preacher knee-deep
in the cold river--
somebody is lifting arms to heaven and shouting Hallelujah!
and afterwards there will be chocolate cake and covered dishes
set out on plywood tables and hymn singing like you never heard
but sleep is coming too...
over my window sill...
covering my eyes with the Balm of Gilead as I tap my toes
against the bed and sing out loud to the sound of the fading music
before sleep takes me again here in the cool deeps of Kentucky
lost in the bosom of Abraham...
Amen, Lord!

Sing on your folks down by the river. Sing you sinners.
Sing on!
You don't see me here in my little room beneath the eaves
where the weasel and stoat move in the dark
you don't know my bankbook or feel my ache in the gizzard
or see me throw the bottle away
YES AWAY! after finding myself in Cairo, Illinois with a
Vote for Mose sign around my neck
Yes, Lord, do you see me here sitting up now, taking nourishment?

Oh yes, oh yes but wasn't she beautiful there at the roller rink
selling them corn dogs and Emu burgers
and yes, choir, stand there in the cold river and lift your arms

to heaven and say there's a man up there somewhere in the dark
who listens to music
and yes dunk them sinners into the moon's reflection
and bring them back again in the same day the same way as Jesus
and John down by the river throwing rocks at rats did
that hot day when locusts and honey were the only menu in town
yes, sinners...do you hear my thumping OK to all that up here
in the darkness and wishing I could have some of your chocolate cake
and eat them wieners and drink all that sauce you got hid
in the brown pot that says baked beans
oh yes, sing to me...sing another verse of that song my mother
sang to me when we sat out on the porch there in Southern Illinois
as the sun went down behind the slag heaps and my father worked
all night in Alton where the river got out of the banks and swamped
everything all right all right all right I hear your songs I
sing them with you all right all right all right
do you hear me singing?
do you feel me thumping my horny feet against the bedstead
do you read my soul there on the curtains billowing and snapping
and popping into my room past my mother's picture on the bureau
and the one picture of Jesus praying in the garden his long
blond hair and blue eyes boring into me?
oh yes

there's the whistle
the train's coming coming coming roaring out of the green forest
heading for that bridge heading for that bridge heading
for the only bridge in Ohio where Cincinnati is
where no one ever lived or will live again
that Cincinnati where Cousin Rose lives and probably awake
right now listening for the train coming bearing her lover
to her as she waits in the dark
singing
oh sing Cousin Rose
sing you sinner
yes sleep, come quickly...let me hum the hymn they're singing
down there by the river and the one Cousin Rose is singing
there in the darkness of Cincinnati--
oh yes...here comes sleep...come on...come on...oh yes!

The Calling

Nublizer Smith looked at the hogs rooting in the mud
and decided he could save them and people both
so he took up a Bible and entered the world singing
hymns and easing burdens by casting out devils
from Tennessee to California and when he reached
Bakersfield he rested with a wife beside a canal
of thin dirty water where he raised hogs and children
and preached in a tent on Saturday nights to people
who crossed plowed ground to get there because
they heard he raised devils right out of you and never
asked a penny to do it so when they found him hanging
by his necktie one dusty windy night someone said
he preached his last or raised the wrong devil and they
tore down the tent and put in a convenience store
where you could get a cold slurpy before you hit
the grapevine on the way to Hollywood and fame
according to the Winns twins Light and Variable
who danced on a raised platform outside the store
with black tap shoes with big white bows and threw kisses
to the eighteen-wheelers hauling vegetables to Oxnard
which the Winns twins thought was probably close enough
and left their black tap shoes with the white bows inside
what was left of the tent where they were told a man
named something-or-other Smith who had the calling
once preached and raised devils and never took a penny.

The Red Chiffon

Sleep wouldn't come, and the 1/2 valium did nothing,
so he looked through the window at the man next door watching television,
his wife gone to bed after changing him.
Then he closed his eyes and listened to cars racing on Market
come back slower, looking for girls.

The red and green blink of traffic lights on the curtains
reminded him of Christmas on the farm when his mother cried
and said he should have been a girl, and years later, woke him
in the night to say his father was dying, and wanted his shotgun
to go to a nephew, who knew how to handle a gun,
and that now she was leaving that hell-hole of a farm
and would never come back.

So she never heard that his house sold at auction,
along with the furniture and all the family pictures;
but the photograph of him hanging in the red chiffon
caught the attention of his Cousin Rose in Cincinnati
who pulled her glasses down off her head and the paper closer.

Melvin Bowles Goes to the Spokane Mall

When Melvin Bowles walked into the store he knew
he was in a strange place. He was not in the Palouse anymore.
He was in a place of people of all sorts who knew what they wore
and the size and what color went with other colors
and whether zipper or buttons would do them.

The sales lady smiled before she even saw him and asked him
his size. "About a 44-29," he said, hitching up his khaki pants.
"You don't want anymore of them, do you?" Melvin Bowles ran
that through his mind trying to find the reply his wife left in it.
"I do too," he said. She stared hard at him as if trying to figure out
if it was a bug on her floor or just lint. "I'll get one of the men
to help you, unless you want to pick up some of the delicates
we have on sale for the Missus."

Melvin Bowles walked out of the store with a bag full of delicates,
all the wrong size and color. He knew the Missus would not like them
because her step-ins were larger and roomier, but he was overcome by
the press of people around him as he fingered each garment, holding each
to his face to see how it slid. That night he held himself ready for her,
trying to picture which silky thing she would wear. He wore nothing,
and squirmed around trying to get warm. It had been a day he would not
easily or quickly forget. He had gone to the Mall and returned with fruits
of the body, the sales lady said. "Go forth and enjoy them!"
The crowd smiled. "Come back and tell us how it went," she said.
The white porcelain doorknob turned, drawing the heavy curtains into
the cold room. He felt the bed give and reached a hairy arm. His eyes opened
wide. It was too dark, but he thought it felt a lot like khaki. Melvin Bowles
was not a lot of things, but one thing he was, was quick. If it slides, it slides,
he said to himself, easing them down, singing something he hoped was opera.

John the Barber
(For Ted)

John says it does me no good to wonder what happened to Larua Lee
Appleton in the 8th grade. "Uh, huh," I say to the mirror.

Mr. Uffleman gave me hundreds if not thousands of sentences to write
because I said I doubted the doctrine of pre-destination, I tell him.
What the hell did I know then, or now, about pre-destination?
          Laura Lee Appleton never thought about pre-destination, I say.
          She just looked up at me with those big blue eyes, butterflies
          coming out of her tulip mouth...
He grins at me in the mirror and turns my head.

I tell him the student I failed in Philosophy of Art is lost to the media-soaked,
wing-nut world he thinks he wants. Make more money. Why? The kid plays
the clarinet like Artie Shaw! Ted says life is a trade off.
          "I cut his hair," he says.
          He dips his comb into something and says, "Money!"
          I wait for what's coming.

          "Raccoons ate my koi last night," he tells me.
"I caught them standing in my pond, each one with a fish."
His scissors go snip-snap in my ear. "You should keep your hair shorter now,"
and raises his eyebrows in the mirror, waiting.
                                        "Go ahead," 1 say. "Take 'em all."
"Life's a trade-off, " he says.

A Lady of Unspoken Graces

"She was not a farm girl," the aunts said, as they took off
their little hats before the mirror. "She should never have
come to the farm." But they could not know that when he held
her close beneath that first Autumn moon, his breath warm against
her neck, she did not imagine shoveling manure out of a barn,
or hosing off hogs caked with mud. Or that the warm breath
on her neck would be from his dog who slept between them, its
one good eye open.

"She was not from around here," the aunts said--and waited
for her to break and run, leaving him to grieve, then find better.
"No one should be surprised if she lacked warmth--if you take
my meaning," they said, and raised their eyebrows as
they pulled on their plastic shoe covers.

"Too thin," one said. "She read books," said the other.
And when his wife died, they came clicking their teeth,
and cooked for him, waiting for him to grow restless in the
winter, wanting someone.

"Someone like the girl on the Havilke place who knows how to
cut horse weeds in the summer and isn't afraid to follow a mule
with the reins wrapped around her waist," they said, adjusting
themselves, smoothing pleats.

They advised light meals, and told him they would see to him,
and nodded to one another, pulling on their little hats in the mirror;
but when he said, "She was a lady of plainspoken graces," they
smiled and said, "Of course she was," and turned to go, their
shadows alert, already moving.

Bond County Funeral
(Southern Illinois)

"We have come to pray him off," the minister said,
and he closed his eyes and began to sing.
When he died on his tractor all but a few said it was God's will.
Now, in the dark suit and Masonic ring, he hunched in his casket
as if still driving.

There were few mourners and those who waited
to carry him out watched warily as the first snow eddied
and drifted around the church, knowing the ruts would freeze
before they got home. The Flat River bunch were there to see it
but left after lunch out on the yard. It was a long drive back
to Missouri they said.

Watching the preacher's mouth work and row,
feeling the heat stick to the roofs of their mouths,
they measured the dead man in their minds, trying to remember him.
Outside, they stamped and blew on their fingers
and watched the winter moon catch in the plum tree orchard
as they followed their silver lanes home.

Watchers

They are all ghosts in the picture albums,
their faces flat and still as they stare
with strange eyes from the photos,
their barns and dead fields behind them.
But I can feel the heat of the long summers
in Turley's Woods and see the crows circle
above the thorn trees; and at the low rumble
of thunder I see them turn to the windows
at the rain, and feel their hands on
the bright porcelain knobs, their shadows
brushing me as they go to the root cellars
for jars or eggs. And I move through my days
and nights waiting for something memorable,
not thinking we stare out from albums-we who
are warm from this spring breath, the watchers
not yet born, not yet finding us.

Crossing Shoal Creek

The letter said you died on your tractor
crossing Shoal Creek.
There were no pictures to help the memories fading
like mists off the bottoms that last day on the farm
when I watched you milk the cows,
their sweet breath filling the dark barn as the rain
that wasn't expected sluiced through the rain gutters.
I waited for you to speak the loud familiar words
about the weather, the failed crops-
I would have talked then, too loud, stroking the Holstein
moving against her stanchion-
but there was only the rain on the tin roof,
and the steady swish-swish of milk into the bright bucket
as I walked past you, so close we could have touched.

Under the Chinaberry Tree

He washed his hair after working
in the silos all day then drove his pickup
into town where he waited in the shadows
for lights to come on before taking off
his clothes under the chinaberry tree
near the window where the woman undressed.
Sometimes wind stirred a branch against
the house and he froze in fear
when she went to the window, seeing only
her reflection in the darkness,
and he held his breath as she stepped
out of her dress and reached her hand
to unsnap her bra, folding her arms before her.
When he could not come to town he imagined
her looking through the window at him,
and when they laughed at his silences
he worked alone at the edge of the upper garden
and at night threw hay down to the cows
who filled the dark barn with their sweet breath.

He watched and waited, crouching naked
under the chinaberry tree until he heard
her come in, parting the leaves to watch
her put necklace and earrings
into the white porcelain box on her dresser,
and once he lay for hours in the notch
of the tree as she sat at her desk,
her back moving gently as she wrote.
When spring came he felt the velvet blossoms
touch his belly and he curled his toes
into the soft wet earth as she slept,
the bedroom bathed in the moonlight
that froze the trees to the window.

When the early snow came he lifted himself
on his toes and watched her peel her stockings
off her legs, slowly, as if she dreamed,
and when she stood naked before the window
he tightened his hands on the windowsill
and felt the wood slice under his fingernails.

When she leaned her body against the cold glass,
her eyes closed, he moved from the shadows
and pressed himself against her, tracing
her arms and legs against the glass,
the chinaberry leaves framing his face
as snow swept through the trees and stung
his bare back and convulsing buttocks,
the white flower unfolding inside him
as she disappeared inside the circle
her warm breath formed on the glass,
her lips parted, her eyes wide in wonder.

Something Different

Their children said to get out of Nebraska and do something
different for your 55th anniversary, for god's sake, and showed
them a postcard of Buffalo Bill standing beside a windmill, so they
went to Detroit Lakes in Minnesota and stayed at a place off the

highway with window air conditioning, which meant you opened
your window, the woman said, and told them to come by the cafe
for some nice gooseberry pie. They unpacked their new suitcases
and took a shower together but could not do more, and laughed so

hard the plastic shower door broke and some water got on the linoleum
floor so they got down naked on their hands and knees with towels
and sopped it up then lay down still laughing on the bed. When the
lady came by for supper they were still asleep so she winked at her

husband and put two pieces of pie in the fridge for later. The next
morning they found them, naked on the bed, their hands touching,
beneath the picture of Buffalo Bill standing beside a windmill.

Blue Lantern Motel
Ashcroft, AZ (Hwy 66)

She shows me a Burma Shave sign
with the initials m.d. carved on it,
but says it's not for sale at any price.
Well, hardly any price...what'll you give for it?

There used to be fun here, she says, and chucks
a salt-cellar at a cat on the counter.
I blow on my coffee and study a picture of four kids
in a convertible. I'm the girl in the back seat
with Donnie, she says. We were going to Flagstaff,
but we never made it. Donnie made it to Viet Nam.

She wipes the counter, watching for the cat.
Coyotes come in from the desert at night,
so mothers sit on porches to watch the children,
she tells me over her shoulder, pushing the cat
out the door with her broom. Can't sleep anyway,
with a hot wind blowing and the Motel sign
blinking on and off in my window.
A fellow from Needles said he could fix it.
He stayed a month. I thought we had something there.

About midnight I raised on an elbow and listened
to her breathing. I looked through the trees brushing
the window at the cat asleep on the hood
of my car. Things blow away, she said.

Over the Cataloochee

- The Great Smokies-

Flying home over the Great Smokies
you try not to remember that the dog
has to be put down and that your daughter
pierced her navel again and her tongue,
preferring to remember the long hike
where we watched for bears and crossed swift
rivers on logs, our boots touching the water
we feared would carry us down to the face-
changing, memory-erasing Gulf. I hope
the forest remembers us, you said, our hands
touching in the dark as we looked up through
the tunnel of trees at the circle of stars,
listening to the night noises.

Flying home, the smoke over the mountains
upwelling beneath the shadow of our plane,
we imagine night falling down the waterfalls
of rhododendron. What are you thinking? you ask.
I think there's an old bear peeing in our footprints right now.
Good, you say. Good.

Country Women

The moon was white and clear in the winter sky over Turley's Woods
and the new ice in the ruts cracked as they eased the casket
onto their shoulders and stepped carefully into the lane.
His wife walked ahead with the minister like country women do,
while the few who turned out for him followed behind,
the faces of the men swollen above their collars,
their wives bent into one shadow behind them.
And when they left him on the little hill and turned away
to town, or farms, leaving the last thing to the two men who waited
beneath the large elm, their shovels bright and clean in the moonlight,
she knew the men watched her and wondered how he died.
But they didn't have to know. Let them guess what took him.
Let them ask the doctor some cold night when they complain of a bellyache
while their woman stands by the kitchen cabinet, smiling,
with the small bottle in her hand; or after the calves are weaned
from their bellowing mothers and they come up from the barn
feeling sick and smelling of milk and hay, to fall asleep with their shirts
stuck to their backs, and wake, feverish in the moonlight to see her
standing near the window, her face pressed against the stiff curtains,
her breath small puffs of cloud on the cold glass, watching
him-let them sleep if they can. Let them all sleep long then.

The Foxes at the Old Irish Cemetery
Killybegs

We hear them bark at evening as we walk
among the stones of the upper garden
where graves swell above the long grasses
that hiss and hiss in the wind off the sea.
Fierce faces look out from photographs we carry,
their barns and dead fields behind them,
but there is no sound or sign to say
that from the green silence of their graves
they hear the waves running up the rocks
or taste moisture on their earthen walls.

We stand in these twilight woods calling
the names aloud, holding back each breath
to better hear, but there are only the breakers,
and the deep-belling of the buoy sounding
in the cold grey sea.

As we pick our way through the winter gorse
home to our own lighted windows,
and sunset breaks into fire over the bogs,
foxes leave their fern-dark holes
among the fallen monuments to lean against the wind,
their ears tipped to catch the voices from the hill
where a lone bird weaves its broken song
among the moon-rinsed trees hiding foxes
moving in light from bark and stone to the sea.

In a Way You Loved
(Killybegs, Ireland)

When you left our cottage at the end of the lane
I thought the flowers would stop you,

bluebells and broom, or the birds would bring you back,
winding their scarlet thread of song around you;

when you broke onto the highroad above the sea
I thought you turned, and I listened for you
in the young alders tossing their leaves white to the wind;
and I smiled in a way you used to love as you vanished
in the hissing grass and a fine mist off the sea.

Millay at the Mall
(for Ted)

When she got on the escalator she noticed the man coming down
and smiled at him then jumped   over   the separator and into his arms

downstairs they sold coffee and rolls
so she had a buttered scone and said it was stale
the manager came out and asked her what she knew about stale scones
and who was that man hanging out of her body
whose legs and arms and hats and dogs and cats and twin moons
were those anyway

we can't have that said a security guard unless you show me your badge
she showed him and he smiled and disappeared into her eyes
          when the band came down the center tootleing and thumping
and asking for money to send them to a parade in NY she squeezed up to
the B flat clarinetist and was quite good at it
people cheered but some led their toddlers away
as she undressed him in mid-march

that night when the stores closed they looked for her in bedding and lingerie
and on sofas and fold-up couches but she was not there--she was upstairs
in the men's department fondling neckties and cooing in the dark
"what fun...what fun... oh the men have all the fun..."
and she tied fourteen together
with iambic knots...the store sold them all...men fell asleep wearing them
because their lives were going on under the ties now...
she had done her work...the Mall is boarded up

the men who live under the escalator rub their greasy hands and intone:
"What lips my lips have kissed and where and why
I have forgotten..."

Underlying Premises

"There's something about you.
Something perhaps in the way of Joyce Carol Oates' underlying premises-
but with perhaps a few too many loose ends."
Her face is half in shadow,
long fingers touching the picture on the Rosy Dresden.
She does not expect a reply.
Then: "Rain is falling on the hydrangea in Cornwall...a rain
Daphne du Maurier must have traced on her window at Ferryside..."

She is silent awhile, eyes closed.
He tries to remember their color, when she sighs,
"Please, let's have no Keats tonight,
certainly nothing of Arnold,--no memories of 'The Dreamy Spires of Oxford'
from that bright windy day we thought ours forever-"
He watches her face appear and disappear in the fading light and wonders
what it is about me-this *thing* that makes life hard, even foreign, she says.
But since he doesn't know, he walks
through "this amber sunstream" she bathes in,
and out the door of their doublewide,
wondering how Keats or Arnold would say "I'm hungry and tired,
and right now cold beer and conversation would be good--"
knowing she will write to her sister Adele that times are grand,
life is fine...civilized, just the way they planned it when they were girls.

The letter remains on the table, unfinished.
She is startled by a dog barking, and thinks of making a drink,
instead she puts on a strand of pearls from her mother and goes to the mirror,
but sees something white, a noose around her neck.
She looks at the picture of Adele and Sir Evan at their home in the Cotswolds
and presses herself against the cold window, listening to the rain sluice
through the plastic rain gutters. "Poor Adele," she says aloud in the dark.
"Poor, sweet...stupid...beautiful...Adele."

kentucky spring

possum hangs on a barb-wire fence
hissing at the rusty barbs dug deep
in his belly
goose him with a stick up off the points
and he drops like a pile of old clothes
face full of teeth and hate chuffing and snarling
dribbing remains of dead bird
stringing out his innards like pearls
on the wet green grass

owl

owl hunch down in old thorn tree
fluff hisself up
rock back and forth like preacher
on a bare black limb

owl shut his eyes tight
trap light & leaves birds dreams & space
no owl there
just a patch on the night

snow come through the trees
somewhere a twig break
wind keep blowin snow keep driftin
owl snap one eye open
ole evil starlight come out the eye like fire
like a tear in a black hole

owl say looky here how I turn my head
get ready mr. mouse under the leaves
get ready little owls down in the bottom
owl and snow soundless shadows over mouse
beneath the leaves

a little bit of chuffin & peckin
then a hoo-hoot like velvet
somewhere in the bottoms
come on daddy owl...come on home...

pond

by the edge of a lovely green pond
a frog muses on life happy in the sun
beating on his pebbly back
his eyes are closed his ugly mouth
works and rows with the last
of a dragonfly waving its wings
like a hanky while just below the surface
of the stagnant green water
a green snake slithers silent and deadly
behind the frog drunk to the shadow
curling around him turning him
upside down sliding him backwards
into the water his lunch dribbing
onto the grassy green water
where three tiny bubbles break
on the surface of the pond
already calming already shimmering
in the late afternoon heat glistening
and lovely on wide-bladed leaves
and delicate ferns bending over
the dark sun-swallowing water

Zoo Story

when the man climbed the concrete barrier and dropped into the pen
of the Great Apes
the crowd cheered
one young mother pulled her toddler away
while another ran for the guard who was smoking
behind the paper maché palm tree
two dark eyes peeped out from a cave
a nurse said it was an ape and this was not
a good thing here
a thin man wearing boots said "from Las Cruces down to Nogales
we got your odd critters...
we just run 'em down in our pickups then blast 'em with our 357's..."

the guard ambled up in time to see the man inside the pen crawling
on all fours toward the great ape who had pushed his massive head and
shoulders
outside his cave
somewhere a whistle blew

a woman shouted something she claimed was Hezikiah 3:12...
something about ape and man and what could only be sin and pain for both...
inside the pen the man stood up and started to remove his clothes
then his shoes and socks
first his shirt
then pants and finally underwear...
small children were held on shoulders of parents
the guard pointed a can of pepper spray at the ape
who watched the man crawl into his cave

guards threw rope ladders over the side of the enclosure...but
no one went down...the man in the suit came up with a clipboard and
went away...
a flashbulb popped and there was a scream from inside the cave...
when reporters arrived it was all over but they asked for

particulars...color...
  "at first we thought he was just loving him..." a woman said
  "my god, he's crushing that man..." another screamed...looking and
      not looking...
the suit with the clipboard wrote something down and went away again...

the ape held the man in one hand and walked up and down the enclosure
then threw the body over the moat scattering the crowd

          "I saw it all" said a man from Nebraska...
"the man with the big hat shot him five times..."
"Ape eats man..." a reporter said... "Dumb-Ass Texan shoots ape..."
      another said...
  "Hezikiah 3:12" someone sobbed...
"I saw it all, and I'm from Nebraska."
The Texan sighted down the barrel of his gun, sucked his teeth and said,
"I've heard of it, but I never believed it."

That night a boy hosed out the enclosure, pocketing the change thrown
at the apes and when he was finished he turned out the lights,
looked at the moon over the big cats' compound and threw his head back
and beat his chest with his hands,
                              thrilled at the sudden flapping of wings
of the exotic birds rising from their nests,
and he held his breath there in the dark as tigers snuffed along their fence,
growling warning--then the sudden jungle quiet--
and the soft lapping at the cold moon floating in their water.

Last Letter from Rose

She told them it was the weather,--rain, sleet and thunderstorms and floods
that carried the eggs out of the hen house that did it,--
but it was the raccoon in the dumpster that drove her out of the country,
Rose said, away from the cow pies in the barn lot in the spring
and the long winters when she used them for stepping stones in the morning,
following her breath to the barn.

It was the raccoon that did it, finally,
Rose said, when she took out the trash and his two beady eyes looked up
at her amidst the cantaloupe rinds and cabbages, always reaching
a nasty little hand up toward her, the opposing thumb
working and snapping as if she were another melon
to snatch into his smelly and steaming den.
So she packed her good dresses, leaving her books, half-eaten by rats,
in the cellar next to the clean jars and brown eggs, and while the hired men
hunched over their biscuits and gravy and he washed his hands at the sink,
his clothes bloody from cleaning the rabbits he shot that morning in the garden,
she gunned the pickup around the white-rock road to the highway,
and it was with relief and a touch of regret
that she left that shit-hole, as Rose called it in her
last letter, that she would not be there to see him when he banged through
the screen door looking for lunch, his clothes wet and heavy from cleaning
the silo, his voice hard and mean as he pulled the cold meat from the ice box,
already reaching for his shotgun,-- the gun she took down and smashed with
a hammer until it barely hung together,
putting it carefully back on the rack over the door,--
-- so she just waved and kept moving, her eyes on the long stretch
of hard road, the horizon squeezing the farm behind her where he stood
in fury at the door, the broken gun at his feet,
the rabbits dancing in the garden,
the raccoon moiling and grunting in his dumpster.

News
(Marmot, Michigan)

Iraq is burning its own people
and someone killed a coed
waiting in line for cheaper gas.
Which story leads, ask the editors.
Lead them both, says a copy boy
still riding his 10 speed. Who is
this boy, asks the Editor. No one
remembers hiring him. Give him
an office and double his salary
so the networks won't get him.
The boy rides home past two dogs
fornicating on the Court House lawn.
He stops his bike and takes a picture
and tells someone without an office
to run it in tomorrow's paper. He did.
The boy lost his job. The Editor reduced
to something. The dogs were available
for comment but didn't. It all took a day.
No one remembers any of it, so someone
nobody hired suggests they do a story
about nobody remembering the story.
The new Editor likes it. Run it, he says.

What are the Odds?

When she said yes, I realized I was in the soup!
Taken: 50 years coming straight down the pike carrying me
along like a leaf, rolling, roiling under and over and through!
Why *Yes?* Surely she had *No* on the tip
of her pink tongue that slid in and out
fast and slow and fast again and again...
There must have been a place along the way when I could have
should have bailed out: sorry, wrong person. Not ready. Things to do,
etc, with great rhetorical flourish as I straightened up in the Ford.
Surely...
Now, fifty odd years later. Surely, she says,
you can find the cupboard in the kitchen where the dishes are.
There are many cupboards in the kitchen, I say, without much heat.
Have you never eaten here these last 50 years? And still don't know
where the dishes are kept? Not a lot of heat there either, but a tang
in the voice, a sigh barely escapes...a lift of shoulders and the drop
that says worlds, as they say on the soaps.

I straighten my back before the mirror, brace
my shoulders, tuck my chin in, knowing the mirror
lies like a rug! Same expression I saw in the rear-view
mirror as I smoothed my mountain of hair and she dabbed
some lipstick on, sans mirror...her father's face pressed
against the steamed window.

Sounds of the little ones (second and third shifts) bring me out of whatever
reverie I slipped into whilst (love that British thing) I stare at the row
of cupboards. She flings a kiss as she goes out the door,
but turns back, head lowered, her mouth pursed for a better one.
A longer hug, close now, feeling the tremor run the length
of the other. The tongues are quiet, but they're ready. What are the odds?

Girls in Their Summer Dresses

Girls in their summer dresses,
like drowsy swans upon a pond
turning their heads as we walk by,
unfold their legs and together sigh
at tiny men in each round eye.

Their dresses billow up and out
like feathers on a sudden breeze,
showing legs and lovely knees,
and every passing man undresses
all the girls in summer dresses
turning their heads as we pass by,
little men in each bright eye.

When it's dark, or nearly so,
and summer girls rise to go,
we circle faster round and round
following their shadows across the ground
and over the hill and out of sight
into memory-enhancing night,
happy to be passing by,
tiny men in each round eye,
and mindful of what each dress caresses,
not a man but secretly blesses
summer girls in their summer dresses.

Rain

When he reached Albuquerque he stopped
under some trees well off the highway and slept
until the rain came harder in the night. He wiped
his breath away from the windshield but the rain
fell harder, filling the old truck with noise until
he covered his head with the blanket he took
at the last minute. It was nothing he really wanted
but he swept it up as he went out the door
for the last time, just in case. It was odd, he thought,
how failed crops and a funeral could be so lost
in his haste, yet his hand could snatch at something
of a life, now over, as if some of it still clung to it.
He drifted in and out of sleep remembering her
coming to the farm for the first time, and how they
clung together when the rains came, and laughed
at the old dog under their bed when the thunder rolled
in the bottoms. And the last thing under the elms,
his neighbors filing in and out of the kitchen with food,
silent, pressing their strange farm bodies against him
at the door, covering their heads against the rain that
ran in rivulets down the new earth in the upper garden.
Sometime in the deep blue of early morning he woke
and got out of the truck, stretched, and drew the wet air
down as far as breath could go, holding it, remembering,
hoping there was something there, something that might grow.

Poplar Street

Down the street a car has crashed.
Ambulances wail somewhere looking for
the address where a man is choking on a fish bone;
the driver curses the traffic and asks the para-medic
if he eats fish.
What kind of fish, he asks the driver.
Any kind of fish. I just want to know if you eat fish.
See that T Bird? I'd give a year of my life and yours too
to drive that baby!
Why fish?
A parade is halted in front of them, the majorette twirling
a baton smiles at them and flips it up and up,
the crowd cranes its neck but the medic can't see it for
the sunscreen. The driver hits the siren, scaring the majorette
watching the baton turn slowly, falling like a wounded chopper
a man in the crowd called a "slick" in Viet Nam.
They snake their way through the parade, blowing kisses to kids,
and turn into the driveway where a woman cries on the porch,
pointing inside, crying in her apron hiding her face, crying.

East of the Mississippi

Corn rows stood in mist like thin ghosts,
their dry husks shivering in a breeze that started
somewhere east of the Mississippi where blackbirds rose
over the tall thorn-trees carrying echoes of voices on Sunday mornings
when we sat in chairs in the yard, listening to cars out on the four-lane
boring through tunnels of Redbud and Maples to Chicago
or farther east to glory or debt, their windows rolled up,
the children asleep past Hillsboro, Litchfield and the towns with no names
save on tombstones leaning into long grass,
and in albums on attic floors, with maybe a news clipping about a man
walking the levee who heard a woman in childbirth in Alton,
where the doctor rolled down his sleeves and said: "It's a girl, I'm sorry..."

and on Monday I watched my father go with the plow,
his jaw tight his hands red from the cold wind
hat pulled low against the sun throwing his shadow across the field
covering me and through the screen door into the cold rooms
until the farm and the animals and the house were dark with his shadow.

Before he turned the horse in the furrow,
the world had turned and I was gone, following my own shadow west,
my mother laid in the spreading shadow of mushrooms under the big trees,
not hearing his call when he turned the old horse,
or reading the notice about his dying and the farm selling at auction,
"with forty acres good for corn, minus the plow
a Golconda man took for his place on the banks of the Ohio."

What They Didn't Say

In Boot Camp we watched films on VD and how to avoid it,
then we got liberty and went to Tijuana anyway
and came back with tattoos in bad places,
some misspelled.

My mother sent me pajamas, but someone found them and hung them
on a pole so the Company Commander would see them and go nuts.
He went nuts.
So we marched for two hours over sea bags and spent two more hours
washing trampled clothes the way he said God intended.

Later we swam until we puked, but I kept swimming
until they said I could be lifeguard and watch the others, but when I hurt
my back in the barracks
I figured my career was just about over, which it was, and so did not listen
to the guys complain of bad sores you know where and how they wished
they had listened to the medics in the worn-out film about
the evils of excess.

But excess, or lack of it, wasn't important enough to keep some of them off
the destroyer that went down three months later,
nor did it change the film recruits saw, showing large pink sores
on places mothers aren't supposed to see;
but the little Lieutenant who knocked on their doors to give them the bad
news about all hands lost in some secret place doing things
requiring no tattoos or grace or courage, apart from just being there,
looked just fine in his penguin suit
with bright eager buttons, with a card in his shirt with what to say
and how to say it and what not to say
and how not to say it.

Fire Fight: 1970

Xuan Loc Province
(for Capt. Mike Doyle)

The only tree left
after the tanks mowed them down
after the big fire to make a laager
the only place to hide with the man
in your arms
bleeding on your chest
calling out something about home ...
one tree
long and dead and full of termites
but safe if you could reach it
fall behind it cradling the man bleeding
on you
his mouth at your ear saying home ...
not hearing the voices
behind the guns
telling you it was your turn
to die
your XO calling, " Gunner, TROOPS'
but you knew it was coming
and pulled the dying man on top of you
feeling embarrassed un-heroic
so you turned him over and laid upon him
like a lover
covering your blood with his
and when it came the dead tree exploded
filling air and bodies with dead tree
then counting the seconds
before the command to reload
running across the fire of grease guns
and RPGs
the other skin and bone
burning through your shirt
something for doctors to separate
after it was over
after the shadows of the whirring blades
drifting over the jungle canopy
taking you to base camp and the other
to die one mile closer to home.

No Time No Place No Way

(Xuan Loc Province, Viet Nam)

It was after his tank exploded
when the RPG ignited the cherry juice
that he knew he was dying and that
he had forgotten to mail the letter
in which he asked her to wait for him
until hell froze over if she loved him
and when he saw the sky turning red
then green from napalm he guessed he
should be glad for that except he was dying
and the tank was a burning hulk around him
the letter still under his pillow on his bunk
back where he was told the mission was a
cinch that no bad guys were around so have
a good time and get to know your tank and
your men and come back for a steak flown in
with a general who wanted to thank somebody
on camera and maybe pin something on him he
could send back in that letter he was writing for
weeks so just run the tanks around and see how
it feels to be standing there half out of the tank
with your own machine gun to fire and two men
to help you win the war one to drive and one to
load and you firing for all you're worth but today
just blow the hell out of trees and anything running
away from you so here he was remembering things
of no worth his skin bubbling his legs caught and bent
forward at the knees his bright machine gun oiled
and perfect and unfired since there would be no bad
guys today and no time no place no way to mail a letter.

A Light Rain Falling

We walked in a park with children calling,
and kissed on a bridge with a light rain falling.
You said you would write, and went to Iraq,
but the letters stopped, and they sent you back
in a box 3X6 with our country's flag
and your name in red on a plastic tag.

We buried you Sunday with your mother crying
when they fired some guns to mark your dying.
A girl from church sang an awful song
and called your name, but pronounced it wrong;
so we went away, with the preacher calling--
we just walked home with a light rain falling.

Baptism

A woman wearing a man's work hat sits in the back
of the country church in Beaver Crossing. After the hymn
she will put on a white robe and bend backwards into the water.
She hopes she will see him the way he was before Iraq,
coming to her across the old bridge, daises in his hand, the sun
in his face. Maybe she will just open her mouth and breathe,
swallow, breathe again and find him, like the letter said,
just coming down the road before the sun exploded.

Winter Liturgies
(Mill Hill Cemetery: Greenville, Illinios)

The wild plum orchard is deep with snow tonight,
and black branches stir their shadows through the drifts
where hedgehogs burrow to find summer's roots.

Gravestones are covered with snow, locking names and dates
away from us as we go from stone to stone to find the child who sleeps
beneath our boots.

"It's like strange winter liturgies, isn't it," you say. "Lovely snow
falling on this awful place, and little voices answering,
like wind.

Isn't there something about your God watching over our going in
and our coming out? Does that include children who sleep in the iron
ground? I've forgotten."

After you find the little stone and press your face against the name,
you will look at me, expecting nothing that will make it right,
and you will turn and go down the hill, your head bare, pushing
through the drifts as if punishing the snow.

Five years have not softened the silence as we sip our tea in the dark
kitchen, waiting for the winter birthday when I will follow you up the
hill and stand beside you as you kneel and rub your fingers raw against
the stones, your grief, and mine, falling on the living and the dead.

Pikes Peak

My father always wanted to drive up there
and see if he could find some land to build
a house on, some kind of view,
something with trees but no "low swag" where water
would gather and rot everything out,
so we watched while he put oil in the '38 Dodge,
cursing the wrench and the oil on his shirt
and the traffic he found as soon as he pulled out
of the driveway of our farm in the quiet hills of Illinois.

We packed and repacked everything so there was not
a space between suitcases and the ironing board and me,
my mother's feet straddling pots and skillets we never used
but once somewhere in New Mexico where a rabid bat flapped
and flopped across our campsite.

Now ready,
he gunned it up Pike's Peak to Paradise
flaming out in pines and snow- capped peaks,
leaving the little tired towns behind as he hunched
over the wheel like he hunched over his biscuits
and gravy on the farm,
my mother standing in the shadows,
pointing at the moon caught in the wild plum orchard,
her finger to her lips lest I say something while he ate,
his jaw muscles working and rowing with bits of cold meat.

Now free of all that,
he guns the Dodge up and up and up
and around, until he feels sick and stops
to throw up on the running board near my
mother's feet,
the pots and pans falling out with a clatter,
hitting his face bent and heaving at the side

of the road.
Never once have I gone back to Pike's Peak
to see if the car I drive will make it without
having to stop for water or air the tires,
or tie something down on top, like a dog kennel,
or the two spare tires in case "there's rocks all over the road
so a man can't even drive up a damn hill on a Sunday..."

The easy part was leaving and arriving;
the middle was sleeping on Baptist Pallets under the trees,
with dogs snurffing around and stars firing in the black sky,
and baloney sandwiches that the dogs got
before I could roll a piece of it up in a slice of white bread
my mother (he called her woman) bought in Texas
as we "got down the line" that stretched from corn to cactus
with never a stop for a bathroom.
"Hold it!" he said,
and I held it until I couldn't, then peed in the ash tray,
swatting a dog away with my left hand, my right hand busy aiming.

Maybe it's not so good to think about what happened to him
after the ocean was always there to look at, and work wasn't
because all he knew was milking and cutting wheat and going with the mule,
the reins tied around his waist as he plowed the upper garden by moonlight
before throwing himself on the bed, still dressed, smelling of the silo
where he went with his little three-legged dog to kill rats.

Maybe it's enough to remember him, hands on hips,
standing on the blue rim of a new world,
the old felt hat pulled down against the setting sun,
the place not yet breaking him with debt and sad dreams,
and my mother gone-

but that would be later, after we stood at sunset, watching the waves breaking
on the rocks, letting the spray wash away some of the Illinois dirt along with
memories of poor crops and bad weather, and the strange farm silences-
my father in shadow, his pants rolled up over his white legs,
running with a flock of thin birds after the receding waves...

Like a White Bird Rising
(Colorado)

When she hiked to the top of the gorge
and read the letter telling her it was over

between them that he was sorry wrong person
and other words to great rhetorical effect

she decided he had made a mistake and spoke
hastily and looked down the thousand feet into

The Black Canyon of the Gunnison when
a sudden gust of wind whipped his letter

from her hand and her off the rock leaving her
with a feeling of wonder watching the mountain

rush past her with pine trees reaching for the letter
rising like a white bird through the closing circle of sky.

October

pale

the night

as

the horse

in the meadow

quiet

over the hedgehen's young

breathing

through the

orange night

the round

white

moon

Van Doren's Snake

Actually, it was my snake. I saw him swimming
under the water hyacinths in a pool far down
the barranca where I sat with my dog,
pretending to be a poet. Wanting to be a poet.
You didn't like the last half of the poem, Mark,
but the first half felt naked without the last half, so
naturally I challenged your not liking the rest.
When your letter came saying I could keep the bad
half if I wanted to, and "besides who the hell am I
to criticize anything," I wanted the postman to
take it back, pretend he made a mistake, wrong
person. Never lived here. No poet at this address.

When you died, I looked at the poem again and saw
why you didn't like the second part. No snake!
Just my reflection staring back, hiding him as he swam
among the water hyacinths, writing S on the sandy bottom.

Winter on Meadow Pond
(Seward, Nebraska)

After the sun slips
over the lip of the prairie
drawing the long grasses'
shadow
over the frozen pond
people return
to their houses
leaving their breath
in the dark trees
and the rabbit
sitting in the middle
of the pond like a white rose

That Slight Edge of Beauty

My father told me I would never see or feel anything
as beautiful as snow falling on the river-and even if I did
I couldn't hold on to it--
that wanting it was like waiting for summer when you're young.
But when I was older I thought I had it when I tried to kiss a girl's eyelashes,
like Peter Lawford did when June Allison raised her pouty lips
in elegant surprise.

There must be a manual somewhere for capturing the beautiful,
with testimonials,
simple illustrations of bolts spiraling into flanges.
But I haven't got the book, the scheme-
and there's always *just this one thing* missing.

My father was right about beauty, and the terrible ache
to see and feel again:
but there's only one time to see snow on the river,
one method for kissing the lashes or fitting the bolt.
But page 2 of 3 is usually missing, or she laughs and runs away.
And that slight edge of beauty between the silent snow
and the undulating wave is all we ever see, all we have to remember.

What They Told Me

At some point, they told me, you will have to grow up
and live your life without us, and they walked up the stairs
into nothingness. They never told me what was at the top
of the stairs, waiting for them in their attic room beneath
the eaves where they shut the door and left me on the couch
in the big room where a banked fire sent puffs of pale smoke
into the black night. It was enough, they told me, that you will
remember us as people who loved you and cared for you in
all weather. You will not be burdened with what must come next,
after we are hurt or infirm.

This you will not see or know about
until it is over and you stand beside the new graves in the upper
garden and sing whatever hymns Rev. Nobs says to sing at the
appointed time when souls are supposed to wing their filmy way
to heaven. There will be some crying and shuffling of feet and
your Uncle Luther will tug at his starched white collar eating into
his neck, and Aunt Eff may be wearing that awful red fox thing
around her shoulders, the one that made you cry, with its little red
beady eyes staring at you. Pay it no mind, and just turn away
as the two men leaning on their shovels do the last thing.

You must come on back to this old farmhouse you love and we loved
and all loved together and eat whatever Cousin Rose from Cincinnati
fixes for you, whether you are hungry or not, and drink her lemonade
just because it will taste good, not because you are thirsty, and when
last light catches fire in the birdbath under the oaks, just sit awhile
with Cousin Rose in the swing and let her tell you how she planted
the clematis vine that grows over the swing so a body could find
some shade in the summer.

Just do these things and try not to lose yourself in grief because we are
in another place, knowing or unknowing, and if there's any truth to
scriptures, a better place-- but a place nevertheless.
Kiss the horses' soft noses tomorrow when you go to the barn to check

for eggs. Hold one to the light and see the red and white life pulsing
just beneath the skin. Then go out the back of the barn into Turley's Woods
and run as far and as fast as you can, and when you can't run anymore,
lie down and look up through the trees, close your eyes and listen to the wind
soughing through the branches and rest. Rest a good long time.
And when you feel better, come on back here and live.

Grandmother

She lay quietly as if she
could wake,
and only pretended
not to know
what our call intended;
but her dress was fresher
than it should have been,
and straighter;
and the eyes were closed
in something more than sleep,
and greater.

A Man and a Woman and a Dog with Pups

On a cold winter day a man and a woman drink hot tea and watch the mother hound, heavy with milk, behind the stove where her pups push against her, straining at the teats, milk running out of their mouths. The man says he left the barn door open, but doesn't think the horse will know, being blind, and pours another cup of tea. When it rains they listen to the water sluice through the rain gutters. It will snow later. Let it, she says, gathering the pups in her apron, stroking the mother's long brown ears. The woman tells her she is a wonderful dog and has beautiful pups and spreads her apron to let the mother worry them back against her body to let them feed. The man and woman stretch out beside her and stroke each other's hair and bodies as rain washes against the house and into Shoal Creek running deep and full to the Mississippi. The rain has stopped, he says, and it's getting colder. It will snow now. This floor is hard for you, she says, cupping her hands beneath his head. It may hurt. Let it, he says.

This Winter Rain

When it rains
the farm sleeps and grows soft
in leaf and land. The cows come up slowly
from the creek.

The horse is in the barn,
nuzzling her oats. Voices are quiet in the house
as if news had come, making them afraid to talk
over the sound of water.

They sit with hot tea,
watching the water run on the kitchen window
and do not speak lest they find they are not safe.

The man is wary, sipping his tea, wondering that
it's come at last, this dissolution after so long a time.
His wife watches him dissolve into shadow and cannot
remember his face. The farm grows soggy and pools form
in ruts. "It may rain all night," he says.

She turns away,
thinking of her dresses in the chest and wonders that
they missed the signs. This winter rain has made it clear,
they think, and will not be the first to climb the stairs to bed.

Ice
(The Snake River at Lyon's Ferry, near Starbuck, Washington)

They told her they would not play on the ice,
but when she looked out the window,
she screamed to my uncle to get out there quick,
then picked up the phone and hung it up and picked
it up again and called the grocery store and hung up

as my uncle came in wet and cold and said it was too late,
that they both drowned quick somewhere under the ice
and would be about Lyon's Ferry by now. My aunt stared

at him then took the broom and beat him on the head
and shoulders, but he just turned his back and let her beat him
until she collapsed in a chair. After the funeral, someone
we didn't know asked why two little girls were playing on
the ice anyway, and who was watching them? From my

chair in the shadows I remember my uncle taking her plate
of ham and potato salad away from her and scraping it into
the dog's bowl, then getting down on all fours and cradling
the dog in his arms, sobbing, his shoulders rising and falling

as people stood or sat with their plates, expectant, until
an aunt said it was a good funeral, and they drew on coats
and mufflers and went out by twos and threes across the yard,
holding pans and covered dishes, putting on rain coats with
one hand. Then the house was quiet and my aunt cut me a piece
of chocolate cake and said to go eat it by the fire. My uncle
was still on the floor with the dog, his shoulders quiet now.

Clematis
(after the funeral) Seward, Nebraska

"Clematis is the vine to plant on arbors
and along a porch. That way you're always
in shade when you sit out on our terrible days."
Heat lightning threaded across the sky and rain
pocked the dust as they swung higher, brushing
the arbor. Her daughter looked toward the barn
where cows moved nervously against each other.
"They want to be milked," she said to her mother.
"He tried to teach me but I could never do it right."

Lying awake upstairs, she listened to the rain pour
off the roof and wondered if she let the dog in,
and if she should give his old shoes to the shelter
in Lincoln. The mud could be knocked off, she thought.
In the night the creek overflowed and puddled against
the tool shed where chickens roosted on the tractor.
She went downstairs and stood on the porch, breathing
the cool wet air, then threw her shawl over her head
and ran to the dog huddled against the barn.
Inside, she smelled the heavy sweet smell of cows,
and looked back to the house, dark, save a pale green light
on her daughter's curtains. Tomorrow I will teach her how
to milk, and though that's not what she's thinking about tonight,
it's what we do. She sat on a bale of hay and pulled the dog
onto her lap and rubbed its ears as the rain fell harder,
hiding the graves by the pond. It's what we do, she said.

Walking Naked in Eden

That's my father and mother walking naked,
memories washed clean of their night-voices
accusing each other, forgetting they tried and failed,
here, where we lose more of each other than we keep.
They are not dead, really, lying side by side on that
Colorado Hill. They're naked in Eden,
taking the first step into each other as air, as light.

This Wanting that Lasts the Years Away

With another winter coming on
the new calf will need a stall of her own,
and the shutters a coat of paint.
The horse weeds by the barn I meant to cut
before you died can wait another year.
The list from friends is long, well-meant:
as were the hugs and food,--and prayers from
your uncle, Bob, or Harmon...
the one badly wounded in Viet Nam.

The preacher did his best;
midges from the creek, circled
like the Cloud of Witnesses in Hebrews, he said;
but the rain came, and we turned away.
Your cousins from Flat River, Missouri did the rest,
with their own shovels, but left before the lunch spread out
on plywood and sawhorses in the barn.

Something was missing in it all, I thought, and kept the truth
away until the last car wound around the white-rock road
to the highway. And when it came I let it wash over me,
determined to feel it all. When it was done with me I saw
it go through the window and up the hill to where you lay
beneath the new black earth, and there it has stayed--
this love, this need, this wanting that lasts the years away.

Morning Greenville, Illinois
(last memory)

My last day on the farm needed something. Conversation.
Talk of the old days. But when we left the barn before dawn
to drive my father's prize Guernseys to water, cicadas had already begun their
thin whine in the trees. When we found the pond, he squatted under a thorn
tree and cut a piece of apple and ate it off his knife and passed the apple
to me, pointing with his knife at the heat lightning over Turley's Woods.
Whatever we had thought to say was lost in thunder in the bottoms, and the
sudden rain pocking the dust on the road where a lone mule headed home,
dragging his broken tether behind him. Water dripped off our hats and ran
down our faces, down our collars, as our faces appeared and disappeared in
the lightning. When we heard the thunder rolling north towards Vandalia,
we uncurled ourselves and slapped our hats against our legs.
Light was coming down the hill through the redbud trees, the air heavy and
sticky. I remember we just looked at each other, then stripped and went in
with the cows, bumping against their huge orange bodies, laughing and
splashing water until we were weak and drug ourselves out and lay on the
bank, searching for words, while dragonflies performed intricate sex above
the gaping mouths of bass, and clouds drifted through the cows, stomach-
deep in the water, shitting and blowing bubbles in the early morning mist.

J.T. Ledbetter lives in Thousand Oaks, California with his wife, Dolores and their chocolate lab, Tess. He is Professor Emeritus at California Lutheran University in Thousand Oaks where he teaches one course a semester.

> My poetry is often about people on small farms who have lost the ability or inclination to talk to each other, having been beaten down by harsh weather, poor crops, and that strange farm silence that covers land and people like a second skin. These memories have left scars that resist stretching but continue to inform my work. My time in Nebraska for graduate school gave me the prairie and quiet people on their weather-beaten farms and reinforced my memories of my birth-home in Southern Illinois for my poems.

BRIAN STETHEM

LaVergne, TN USA
01 October 2010
199314LV00003B/19/P